WHO STOPPED THE SALE?

Learn to master the art of sales, become an essential asset, and close more business.

RICHARD F. LIBIN

PRAISE FOR WHO STOPPED THE SALE?

"Richard Libin is a sales and marketing innovator, a man who is forever studying the way we perform in the workplace, and challenging us to find a way to do it better. In *Who Stopped the Sale?* he shows us that poorly managed sales systems and a careless approach to customer service, can hurt our bottom line more than our most feared competitor. He tells us, with insight and common sense gathered from years of observation and experience, how to stop competing with ourselves."

Jack Warren, Owner, Warren Business Graphics

"Full of simply stated wisdom, *Who Stopped the Sale?* should be a primer for everyone who has contact with customers, from the receptionist to management, and most important the sales team."

Elizabeth Beddow, Proprietor, Fiamme Restaurant & Bar Los Angeles and the award-winning Golddigger Vineyard, Founder LiveWire Integration Consultants, Inc.

"An extremely useful and informative book based on a lifetime of experience – Richard Libin shows us that to be successful the new era of sales and service requires a new mindset, one that has to be constantly refreshed both personally and professionally through continuous education."

Mary Beth Aufmuth, Author of A Study Guide for An Introduction to Sociology, President of the Cleveland Diocese's Council of Catholic Women

"Who Stopped the Sale?" is a valuable book that is clear and to the point about a salesperson's job – to facilitate a sale every time you encounter a prospect. It gives practical wisdom in an easy-to-read format."

Dr. Richard Levin, Executive Coach, Leadership Developer, Television Commentator, and Newspaper Columnist, President, Richard Levin & Associates, Wellesley, Massachusetts

"Great content! Great format! *Who Stopped the Sale?* is an easy-to-use, step-by-step approach from a pro who knows what he's talking about on the subject of how to sell more and make customers happier at the same time."

Steve Finlay, Senior Editor, Wards Dealer Business magazine

"This book blends common sense that many in sales have forgotten (or abandoned) with unique insights to chart a clear course for sales success regardless of the product, service or climate. It's a must read for any sales professional."

Kenneth Grabot, Senior Executive, motion picture industry

"Who Stopped the Sale? makes an impression on everyone in business, whether or not you are in sales. This book, coupled with consistent application of its principles, ongoing education and hard work, helps business people refocus on the customer while providing a guide for success from the first customer contact through the entire process."

Joanna Burke, Henry J. Burke & Sons Funeral Home

ISBN-978-0-9883168-0-5

Automotive Profit Builders, Inc.
P.O. Box 2011
Natick, MA 01760

Telephone: (508) 626-9200
Email: rlibin@apb.cc

Web: www.whostoppedthesale.com,
www.richardlibin.com and www.apb.cc

First edition published 2010.
Second edition published 2013.

Editing: Bonnie Quintanilla
Production: Corridor Communications, Inc.

In memory of my father, George M. Libin, founder of Automotive Profit Builders, Inc., a pioneer in the automobile industry.

I dedicate this book to my wife Cathy, to my daughter Jennifer and to my son Michael. You have always supported me with confidence, no matter where life's path has taken us.

You are my inspiration.

"Ongoing education represents an opportunity to grow people, profit and performance."

TABLE OF CONTENTS

PREFACE

In a perfect world, this book would never have been written. Yet, nearly every day I receive emails like the one below that only further emphasizes that we have lost touch with the basic art of selling. Most of these emails come from people who have read my articles or who have participated in my courses.

From: Keith A.
Sent: June 10, 2008
To: Richard Libin
Subject: Ward's Dealer Business

Dear Richard:

I recently read your article while waiting in my dealership for my car to be serviced. As a salesperson myself (electronics) I couldn't agree with you more.

I have to say, however, that not much has changed in the NY metro area. To wit:

I recently helped a friend buy a new Toyota (Five Towns Toyota) . During the test drive, the salesperson alluded to the fact that the front seats reclined and that we could have a great time with the girls. I told him we were gay (we're not) but the blood draining from his face was a priceless reaction! Back at the dealership, he asked, "What do I have to do to put you in this car today?" I swear, no kidding, he actually said that. After negotiating, he whined that "Any more customers like you and I'll be out of business!" and "I'm not making a dime on this!"

A good friend, recently divorced and armed with a large cash settlement, walks into the local Volvo dealership (Karp Volvo). "I hear Volvo's are safe cars, what do you recommend?" Salesman: "Well, what do you want? S60, S30?" Friend: "I know nothing about them." Salesman (big sigh): "Let me show you what's in stock." He takes her to a car on the lot, which is locked. He shrugs, and then his cell phone rings. It's his girlfriend. They argue while making dinner plans. Meanwhile, the car remains locked. The salesman ignores her. She walks.

She goes down the road to the Chrysler dealership (Conway Motors), gets treated fairly and with respect, and walks out with a new Sebring and a new Liberty, paid for in cash, by the way.

When will these guys learn?

Best regards,

Keith A.

P.S. Feel free to use these stories in your seminars/articles. You must be busy!

When, indeed! Think for a moment. In the last 30 days have you had an encounter with a salesperson that made you feel the same way? I am 100% certain that everyone reading this book will say, "Yes." Furthermore, if you ask your friends, family and colleagues, they all will say "yes" as well. **As a salesperson, the question to ask is how many people answer, "yes" to this question while thinking about you?**

More often than not, like the Volvo salesperson in this example, salespeople stop sales, and many do so without ever knowing. This book will turn your idea of "selling" upside down, redefine your job, and put you on the path to facilitating a sale every time you encounter a prospect.

The information here is proven to work, but only when embraced with an open mind and the understanding that success in sales is a process nurtured by continuous learning and improvement. The first step? Be willing to recognize that you, too, stop sales.

AUTHOR'S NOTE

Throughout this book I will be using the words "opportunity," "customer" and "client." For clarity, I will define them here.

Opportunity: An opportunity is any person who calls, emails, or walks into a store. Everyone has the potential to be converted to a customer. Opportunities may also be considered shoppers.

Customer: A customer is an individual who makes a single purchase and leaves. Customers are also considered buyers.

Client/Clientele: A client is a customer with whom a salesperson has fostered a long-term relationship. Clients not only ask for a specific salesperson, but also trust that salesperson's advice. And, knowing their clients, the salesperson is able to sell them a product or service, which may cost a bit more, but meets their needs so precisely, that there is little room for discussion. It's carefully cultivated trust that allows the salesperson to secure referrals and higher value and higher volume sales.

"The customer has the power in the relationship."

INTRODUCTION

SOMETHING'S DIFFERENT

Something's different. You can feel it, but you're not exactly sure what it is. Is it the economy? Have the rules changed? No. The difference is, that everyone is so distracted looking for a magic potion that they've forgotten, or worse, they ignore, the basics. Even within the same company salespeople have different perspectives and approaches. Take two employees who work for the same airline as ticket agents in two different locations, ask them what business they are in. I'm confident that you will get completely different answers. For example,

"We are in the transportation business."

"We are in the customer service business."

Both may be correct. However, any salesperson or manager in any business or market who doesn't believe that they are in the customer service business doesn't understand the new rules of business. Everyone is in the customer service business. And, even more important to accept, the customer has the power in the relationship. Gone are the days when a bank, for example, could keep customers for life simply by offering toasters or even better loans. Today, people and businesses change banks as often as they buy new cars.

Buying decisions are no longer driven by quality and price, but by these three concepts:

1. Customers make the rules. They have choices. They are not reluctant to walk away and shop your competition.

2. Your competition has changed. Competition is everywhere. Customers will compare your service to their most recent "best" experience, regardless of whether it was at a hotel or lawn mower store. It's about how customers felt and how they perceived you or how your team treated them. You are in the service business, regardless of your product.

3. Quality and features are the expectation. Selling on quality is like a restaurant advertising that every diner gets food. It's a given. If your product or service doesn't have exceptional quality and features, get out of the game now; you don't stand a chance.

In the 30+ years I worked with my father and now as president of Automotive Profit Builders (APB), I have found one precept to be absolutely true regardless of what product or service you sell or what marketplace you play in: how well you believe you are doing doesn't matter. It's the perception of the customer that makes the difference. To say it another way, your internal standards must be as high as or higher than those of the marketplace.

Yet, more often than not, salespeople and their management stop the sale long before it ever gets off the ground. My work providing counsel to hundreds of companies proves that with the right education and a commitment to continuous improvement, salespeople no longer have to be their own worst enemies.

The first step is to understand the behaviors that stop the sale before it starts. Later, we'll examine how to put yourself in your customers' shoes so you can convert customers to clients, and finally, how to build an environment suited to the new rules of business.

"My job is not to sell, but to help my customers buy by helping them find the exact product or service that meets their needs."

PART ONE:

THE NEW WORLD OF SELLING

"Everyone is looking for someone they can trust, someone they can have confidence in."

CHAPTER 1

WHAT'S MY JOB?

- Gone is the era of the stereotypical salesperson that focused on selling as fast as possible, regardless of the customers' needs.

- Gone are the days of the "top secret" sales contest where the winners kept their jobs.

- Gone is the idea that the sales force can compensate by sheer "salesmanship" or by showing some value-added goodies to swing a deal.

- Gone are the days when the ideal salesman looked like Clark Kent transformed into Superman – muscular, a winning smile, six-feet tall.

In today's world of business, with technology that makes information available 24/7, the reality is that customers just don't need salespeople – not the way they have in the past. Traditionally, salespeople have always done two things for their customers: communicate information and quickly sell products and services. These two basic functions no longer provide value.

Yet for many, these functions – an ability to communicate information and close deals – remain their core approach, making them virtually obsolete. As a salesperson, how do you define your job? If you believe that your job is to give information and close the deal, then you should ask yourself if you have the ability to change.

Today's salesperson has a job profile that can be defined in three simple functions:

1. Salespeople are responsible for helping customers select the right product or service.

2. Salespeople must help a customer fall in love with their selection.

3. Salespeople must convert customers to clients.

Let's examine each of these functions more closely.

Salespeople Are Responsible For Helping Customers Select The Right Product Or Service.

- To do this, salespeople must demonstrate a sincere interest in each individual opportunity, and work to gain information and help find the right product or service. The formula for success is straightforward: 100% Attitude + 100% Effort + 100% Performance = 100% Results. Salespeople must...

- Be 100% present and work with a single-minded focus for each customer.

- Ask probing questions to develop an understanding of the customers' unique needs, wants and desires. It's not about what the salesperson thinks; it's all about what the customer thinks.

- Listen, learn and empathize with the customers, understand problems from their point-of-view and discover essential details in order to successfully guide the selection process and find an exact fit.

- Help the customers "try it on." Throughout the introduction and including a demonstration, if applicable, the salesperson should guide customers as they experience the features that will satisfy their needs, wants and desires.

- Introduce customers to the rest of the "family." Give them a tour of the business or store, introducing them to all the managers, and explaining that everyone is here to take care of all their needs.

- Begin to convert customers to clients.

Salespeople Must Help A Customer Fall In Love With Their Selection.

If a salesperson is truly helping a customer buy, the customer will develop an emotional bond with the product and service and virtually fall in love with it, so much so that they can't let it go. Have you ever bought a pair of shoes that you just had to wear home? If so, the salesperson succeeded in helping you fall in love with the product.

When this happens, price becomes a secondary concern. Today, any discussion or negotiation of price should always come last and always take the least amount of time. This is not to say that price is not important. However, when time is spent on the selection process, and an opportunity falls in love with a product or service, price is rarely the reason a sale is lost. When a salesperson sells price, or pre-qualifies a customer based on their budget before landing the customer based on needs, wants and desires, then price becomes the primary issue.

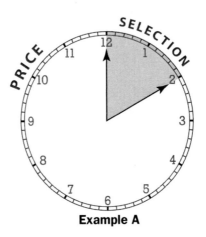

Example A

In the past (Example A), in a 60 minute transaction with a customer, a mere 10 minutes might be spent on selection and 50 minutes spent negotiating price. The salesperson's primary goal was to close a sale as soon as possible, not to help the customer find the right product or service, one they can fall in love with. This approach today makes it easy for the customer to walk away and is a sure-fire formula for disaster.

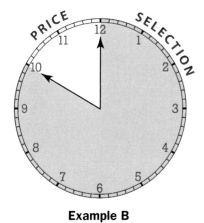

Example B

In Example B, the ideal approach for selling today, the salesperson spends 50 minutes of the hour helping a customer select the right product or service and only 10 minutes on price. Here the emphasis is on building a relationship and helping the customer make a selection by listening to his needs, wants and desires. Not only will this approach help close more sales and create greater customer satisfaction at the time of the purchase, but it will have lasting effects as the delighted customer raves about his experience, refers his friends and family, and ultimately becomes a client.

Think about how most women purchase clothes. A woman goes to a dress rack, flips through the dresses until one catches her eye, she holds it up, feels the fabric, looks over the style, tries it on and checks to see how it looks in a mirror. Only then, after she's selected it as the right dress and has fallen in love with the look and feel, does she look at the price tag.

Price should be raised only after customers feel at home and have built a strong emotional bond with a product or service, the business and the salesperson.

It is the salesperson's job to make sure that customers understand and believe that the price is worth the value of product or service they selected, that the price fits a customer's budget, that payments are acceptable. If the salesperson has truly mastered these first two job functions, price almost becomes immaterial.

Salespeople Must Convert Customers To Clients.

The salesperson's job does not stop at the close of the sale, yet most customers never get a follow up call or any form of contact once they leave a store. Why? For most salespeople, it is fear of rejection, not knowing what to say and not knowing how to say it. Follow up contact is essential and can be successful if these steps are followed:

- Have a purpose – understand the outcome you want from the call. Is it a referral or additional sales, perhaps?

- Plan what you will say – script it out – but, never read the script once you are on the call.

- Think about and plan how you will communicate it.

- Be prepared for the customer to lead you down another path and be ready to bridge back to your purpose.

Consider this example:

a. Desired outcome: referral/lead and relationship building

b. What you want to say: Did your friends or family like your purchase?

c. How will you say it: When did you first wear your new suit to work? (In this case the salesperson knew why the suit was being purchased, which is his first job function.) What did your friends and colleagues think about it? How did it make you feel? Did anyone ask where you purchased it? Would you mind if I gave them a call?

The goal is to make the follow-up a continuation of the positive purchasing experience. Starting a conversation that gets customers excited about their purchase all over again can lead to a referral to a friend who might be looking to do business with you. It's the ABC of selling – Always Be Closing.

Here's how it works when all three functions are executed properly.

I used to buy my suits from a guy named Ed who worked in a large men's shop. Each time I'd go in he'd say, "Good morning Mr. Libin, what's the occasion you are shopping for today?" As we talked about my business, family and the suit, he'd weave in questions that helped pinpoint my exact needs, wants and desires, and listen carefully to my answers. Then, he'd find a suit and I would try it on.

Ed would button the jacket, adjust the shoulders, pull down the sleeves and fuss over it until I was feeling pretty good about it. Then he'd say, "No, that's not the right suit for you." He'd find another suit, repeat the process, and I'd feel even better about it. Then we'd close the sale – but only after he introduced me to the tailor just in case I ever had a need. Ed created a "want" in the first suit, took it away and created an even stronger desire by finding the *right* suit for me. Price was never discussed. A day later I would get a call asking what my wife thought about my new suit.

So how do you start? With one essential first step: accept the fact that your job is not to sell but to help customers buy. Make it your mantra; say it, repeat it and come to believe it. Every day when you get out of bed, and several times during the day, repeat to yourself, "My job is not to sell, but to help my customers find the exact product or service that meets their needs and in doing so, make sure their experience is positive."

It's about adopting the right attitude every single day. When you do, you will have started your journey on the road to winning, and along the way, you'll help your colleagues change their mindset as well.

Once you embrace this precept, the tools in this book will help guide your journey and prepare you for the constant change that we can expect everyday in sales. Remember, "a winner always finds a way; a loser finds an excuse."

>
> *"People love to buy things, but they hate the feeling of being sold."*

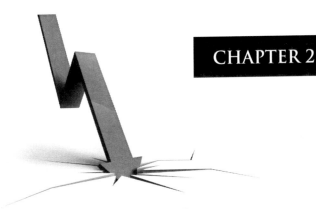

CHAPTER 2

CREATING SALES SELECTION SPECIALISTS

Let's review. True or False: A salesperson's job is to sell products and services.

FALSE!

A salesperson's job is to help customers buy the right product or service, the one that fills their needs, wants and desires; not simply to close a sale. When salespeople understand this, price becomes a secondary issue.

Businesses and stores spend trillions of dollars annually on advertising, incentives and promotions simply to attract buyers. Yet, salespeople who focus on selling, meeting quotas and landing the immediate sale, often succeed at only one thing: **turning buyers into shoppers**. As a result, management believes their teams don't perform, frustrated salespeople blame the lack of incentives, poor market, or their management, and a negative attitude permeates the entire business.

Through extensive experience and research, I have found that buyers who leave businesses without purchasing usually describe their *experience* as uncomfortable, either because the sale is not moving in a positive direction, the salesperson is not connecting with them, or they are not being shown a product that meets their needs.

People love to buy things, but they hate the feeling of being sold. What customers want is a business or retail culture that makes buying a comfortable experience where sales professionals give them quality time. Everyone is looking for someone they can trust, someone they can have confidence in. Most opportunities walk into a business or store ready to buy. The salesperson doesn't have to persuade them; he just needs to help them find a product that meets their needs.

Buyers rate the helpful attitude of the salesperson as one of the major reasons why they purchase. No one ever talks about being "sold" a product by the efforts of a persuasive salesperson. They describe how a salesperson guided them through to a *"buying"* experience. When this happens, sales increase and satisfied customers make referrals and return for additional services or accessories. This is a true measure of *value*. These customers are on their way to becoming clientele.

Beware of these three traps that can turn buyers into shoppers.

One: Killing The Sale Before It Ever Gets Started

> Salesperson: "Hi, can I help you find something?"
> Buyer: "No thanks, I am just looking."
> Salesperson: "Ok, let me know if you need help."
> Buyer: "Ok."

Instead of asking a question that everyone knows will be answered with a "no" or a simple shrug 90% of the time, the salesperson should ask a question that starts to build a rapport and engages the opportunity in conversation. Introduce yourself. Find out the customer's name. Then, find out how you can assist. Offer to help the opportunity make a selection and guide him in his decision through thoughtful questions that provide insightful information. This will be explored more in Chapter 4.

Every Wal-Mart store has a greeter stationed at the entry door of every single store. As soon as a customer walks in, the greeter engages them in a non-threatening or pushy manner. They smile, say "Welcome to Wal-Mart." Their job is to build rapport, put the customer at ease and make it easy for them to ask for help.

Before your next customer walks in, think about how you will engage them. What will you say? How will you put them at ease? What question will you ask? Always put yourself in a position to win, not in a position where the customer can make you lose. We will explore this in more depth in Chapter 4.

Two: No. Don't. Won't. Can't.
Negative Attitudes Bring Negative Results.

Buyer: "I like this product, but I want it in silver."

Salesperson: "Silver is on back order right now and I can't get it for a month or two. You probably don't want to wait, do you? Let me show you the gold. It's metallic and has the same rich look as the silver. You won't know the difference."

Buyer: "Hmmm, I really wanted silver...let me think about it. I'll be back."

How many times have you heard that one? Einstein said it best, "The definition of insanity is doing the same thing over and over again and expecting different results." In this case, the salesperson stopped the sale with negative responses. Instead of pushing the gold vehicle, the salesperson should have presented all of the options. Then the opportunity could have made an informed selection. He may have picked his second favorite color – perhaps red, ordered the car in silver, or opted to think about it and come back.

Three: Buy Now vs. Buy

> Buyer: "I am looking for a full size SUV with 4-wheel drive. I have six kids!"
>
> Salesperson: "I don't have one of those in stock right now, but I have crossovers. They are similar and provide virtually every feature you can find on an SUV. Let me show you one of these. I have one that is a bit smaller, but it should work. And you can drive it off the lot today."
>
> Buyer: "Thanks anyway, I think I'll look around a bit."

In this last case, the opportunity leaves and becomes someone else's customer because the salesperson was more concerned about closing the deal quickly – now – than with helping the customer find the right vehicle and falling in love with it. While the crossover may have been similar, a smaller vehicle would not have met the needs of a family of six…their friends and gear! We will explore this in greater depth in Chapter 5.

Each of these traps resulted in buyers becoming shoppers who left and most likely went to a competitive store. In each case, the salesperson didn't build rapport by asking thoughtful questions and listening to the answers. The salesperson was more interested in selling than in helping a customer select the right product, the one they actually needed, wanted and desired. Falling into these traps causes buyers to become disenchanted or frustrated. Even though the buyer will promise to "think about it and come back," more often than not they were just "being nice" and had no intention of returning. Instead, these shoppers turn to alternative stores or the Internet until they find exactly what they want to buy or until they find a salesperson with whom they want to do business.

A few simple changes, especially in attitude, will help avoid these traps and bring about enormous rewards in terms of performance and the bottom line. With the right attitude, skill and patience to ask meaningful questions, listen, and focus on helping the opportunity select a product or service, no one will ever leave your business as a shopper, but as a buyer – whether they purchase now or later. Think of it this way: **A salesperson's job is not to sell, but to help customers buy.** Only then can you focus on building long-term clientele.

"A salesperson approach impacts the ability to deliver 100% more than any other factor in sales."

CHAPTER 3

100% OR...
WHY BOTHER?

A salesperson's approach to work can be one of the most telling aspects of how he is regarded by customers and co-workers. Think of someone you've worked with who didn't bring a positive attitude or put forth the effort and performance you expected. Did he follow the company's processes or just think about the shortcut to results? How did you feel every time you had to work with him? A salesperson's approach defines who he is and impacts his ability to deliver 100% more than any other factor in sales.

The key to maximizing results for customers, employers and themselves is to *give* 100%. The formula never changes:

100% Attitude + 100% Effort + 100% Performance = 100% Results.

ATTITUDE

Each day every person makes a choice about how they intend to approach their day. They can get up and embrace the day positively or grumble about the awful day ahead. In either case, their attitude becomes a self-fulfilling prophecy. Maintaining a positive attitude is the first step in keeping buyers and converting them to customers and eventually to long-term clientele. Focusing on the negative – lower sales, higher overhead, problems with the economy, or even a "bad morning," – shifts attitudes and negatively impacts performance.

Consequently, opportunities don't receive attentive service, don't enjoy the experience, and sales fall. Managers look at the salespeople and think, "I don't have a very good team," or "Don't they know how to close a deal?" Salespeople can be heard lamenting, "We have more people coming in, but they don't really want to buy, not what we have to sell, how can I make any money?"

Not only do negative attitudes telegraph to customers through body language and words, but they re-enforce the importance of closing the deal immediately versus finding the right product for each customer. Words like "**No, Don't, Won't,** or **Can't**" slip into a salesperson's vocabulary more frequently and only serve to help kill the opportunity.

Consider the impact word choices have on attitudes. Stop using words like "shoppers," people who visit stores in search of articles to

Half Price Books
1835 Forms Drive
Carrollton, TX 75006
OFS OrderID 24141289

|||||||||||||||||||||||||||||||||||

SKU	ISBN/UPC	Title & Author/Artist
S331769822	9780988316805	Who Stopped the Sale?
		Libin, Mr. Richard F.

SHIPPED STANDARD TO:
Richard Hill
2025 ARROW CT
EL CAJON CA 92019-4226
qg5mdg6p70pjbx7@marketplace.amazon.com

ORDER# 114-57
AmazonMarketp

or your order, Richard Hill!

s to sell your books, music, movies games for cash.

Shelf ID	Qty	OrderSKU
BUS 4.5	1	

32-7596202
US

buy, or "customers," individuals who make a single purchase and leave. True sales professionals think of their customers as clients, people with whom they should foster a long-term relationship.

PERFORMANCE

First, set goals. Know what the objective is and what has to be done every day to achieve it. Is it calling three clients? Setting two appointments? Writing five thank you notes? Attending a networking event? What has to be accomplished consistently every day, 100% of the time? Performance is defined by Webster's as "the execution of an action." Once goals are set, it is the responsibility of each individual to perform them fully, 100%. If you commit to making three calls, make them. Period. If you don't you only hurt yourself, your performance and ultimately your attitude.

EFFORT

Webster's defines effort as "a conscious exertion of power; hard work; a serious attempt." Once goals are set, every salesperson must give 100% effort toward achieving them. Turn off Facebook or Twitter, skip the personal calls, and focus on achieving the goals. With 100% effort, achieving 100% performance is simple.

RESULTS

Everything a salesperson does impacts his results. Bringing a 100% positive Attitude, adding 100% Performance and 100% Effort will bring 100% Results. If you're having a "bad" day, stop and *honestly* check these three factors – attitude, performance and effort. Then, make adjustments and go after the results.

―――＊―――

*"Never ask a question
unless you know
the answer."*

―――＊―――

CHAPTER 4

ASK THE RIGHT QUESTIONS AND LISTEN!

Doing business starts with a salesperson's understanding that his primary responsibility is to select the right product for each individual buyer. How will you know when that happens? Only when customers are reluctant to let the product out of their hands. But how does a salesperson get them to that point? First, every employee, not just salespeople, must make a commitment to actively listen to customers. Then they must learn how to ask questions that are direct, but non-confrontational or pushy and that draw out specific information that build on the salesperson's ability to move the process forward. A young man's experience at Hugo Boss provides an example of how asking the right questions can lead to a sale.

> Salesperson: "Welcome, I'm Tom Evans and my job today is to help you select a suit (*this could have been any product or service*). Is that ok with you?"

Ten times out of ten times the response will be "Yes." This simple change in approach opens the door and allows salespeople to use well-honed sales techniques to steer the conversation through browsing, into a demonstration or fitting, and ultimately to a sale, whether or not the sale is made immediately.

Salesperson: "What's the occasion you are looking for?"

Buyer: "It's for my prom, but I don't think I can afford to purchase here."

Salesperson: "Well, let's just see what size you are to be sure you get the right fit when you do make a purchase. Were you thinking about a color or style other than one you already own – what were you leaning toward?"

Buyer: "Ok," as he starts to be measured. "I want to get a black suit that will work for other occasions, too. The suit I have is green – I like it, but it's limiting."

Salesperson: "Good idea. For the prom, do you know the color of your date's dress?"

Buyer: "Blue, sort of a sky blue."

Salesperson: "Why don't you try this one, just to see how it fits? Do you need to find a matching tie and shirt - what color were you thinking about?"

Buyer: As he heads toward the dressing room, black suit in hand, he says, "I was thinking about white. On the tie, I don't need to match the blue, do I?"

In this case, the salesperson engaged the young man by attentively listening and offering to help him, regardless of when or where he buys the suit.

Even though the salesperson knew the young man looked dashing, upon exiting the dressing room, he made adjustments to the sleeves, collar and other parts of the suit to show a real interest in the end result. He continued to engage his client offering tips like showing a quarter inch of sleeve below the jacket cuffs or never buttoning the bottom button on the jacket, the kind of shoes, belt and socks to wear, and ideas on how to make his date feel special. The young man enjoyed the experience, gained confidence, felt like a million dollars and left having purchased the suit from a sample sale that fit his budget as well as a shirt, a tie and cologne.

"Asking the right questions encourages customers to answer in a way that gives direction on how the salesperson can help resolve uncertainties, and in the end, sell the product."

Asking specific, well-thought-out questions allowed the salesperson to learn about the type of suit the buyer was looking for, the occasion, the customer's preferences for style, comfort, color, etc., and what he liked or disliked about his current suit. It also helped him build rapport and key in to what the buyer really wanted: confidence that he would make a good impression with his date. Only then could the salesperson find the right suit and ask the buyer to try it on. The question of price essentially became immaterial.

This approach only works if a salesperson truly listens to the responses. For example the following exchange, in a previous store, turned the young man from a buyer into a shopper:

> Salesperson: "This suit looks great – are you happy with the selection?"
>
> Buyer: "Well, actually, it feels really big."
>
> Salesperson: "That's the way they are supposed to fit, it's perfect, let's ring it up."
>
> Shopper: "I think I'll look around, can you hold this for me? I'll be back."

Why did the opportunity give that response? The attentive salesperson will understand that the opportunity had not truly made a final selection. Until this happens, nothing – even an exceptional price – will ever truly satisfy the opportunity, and will ultimately convert the buyer into a shopper who goes to competing stores and businesses.

By asking qualifying questions, a salesperson will learn immediately about the type of product, potential uses, the style and feeling the customer is seeking. These questions help the salesperson understand the direction to go with the product selection. It allows the salesperson to present the right solutions and to steer the customer into "trying it on." Asking the right questions encourages customers to answer in a way that gives direction on how the salesperson can help resolve uncertainties, and in the end, sell the product. Keep in mind, the salesperson is an agent of the customer and an agent of the store – a double agent.

Never ask a question unless you know the answer. This might sound foolish, but think about it. If you say, "May I help you?" to a customer entering a store, nine times out of ten his answer will be, "No." Asking the right questions will provide clear information that is needed to direct the sales process. The right questions will also help build rapport, the first step in converting customers to clients. Remember it's not what the salesperson says, but how he says it.

———•———

*"No matter how hard the
push is to buy NOW, the result
is the same: if it is not the right
product for the customer, nothing
will make them buy,
not even price."*

———•———

CHAPTER 5

DOING BUSINESS OR DOING BUSINESS *NOW!*

Have you ever known anyone to simply wake up one morning, grab a cup of coffee and decide, "Today I am going to go spend $50,000 on a car, boat, stock, trip or home...?" No one in their right mind makes high value purchases like these spontaneously. They spend time researching and then look for a salesperson to help them with the selection process, and, finally, with price. Think about it, how long did it take to buy your first house?

Traditional sales methods have always focused on closing the sale, *NOW*. As a result, many opportunities feel pressured and uncomfortable with the salesperson, and by default, with the business or store, and they leave. Buyers become shoppers and the business loses opportunities to create long-term clientele who will return time and again. The question becomes, "is your business or store seeking to do business or simply to do business *NOW*?" What is the goal? The answer should be, "to build clientele that will return and shop repeatedly, not simply to close a quick sale *NOW*." Keep in mind that if a client doesn't do business with you *NOW* it doesn't mean he won't do business with you later.

A serious misperception in the sales world is that business must be transacted immediately – *NOW*. As a result, sales professionals – many of whom really know better – repel customers by peppering them with questions about price and closing the deal, ultimately ending with "What would it take to buy the product *NOW*?" No matter how hard the push is to buy *NOW*, the result is the same: if it is not the right product for the customer, nothing will make them buy, not even price.

In the sales world, there is only one true definition of *NOW*. It's when the customer is ready to buy and take the product home.

All successful sales are made up of three elements:

1. Helping customers select the right product that meets their needs, wants and desires.

2. Earning their business by creating an experience that makes customers feel like they are at the right business and working with the right salesperson.

3. Finding the right price.

Let's apply this to customers shopping in a clothing store. If an outfit is appealing, a customer takes it to the fitting room and tries it on. If the look, feel and fit are right, then the customer considers price. Price often is the last consideration for something that fits right and looks good.

It is the same with virtually any sale: a customer is interested in the appropriate product, the right features and fit, and then the price. *NOW*, that artificial sense of immediacy has nothing to do with the sale. It has no place in the sales process and is an impediment more than an aid.

Again, the question becomes: Is your business looking to do business or simply looking to do business *NOW?* When an opportunity walks in, the goal should be to develop, gain and then retain his business. Whether he buys today or *NOW*, next week or next month doesn't matter. What matters is that buys, that he buys from you and that he does so repeatedly.

If a buyer chooses to consider a purchase, it is imperative that the salesperson gain enough information before the buyer leaves to maintain contact, especially in the first 72 hours after the visit.

1. Minimally, the salesperson should collect and record standard, detailed data; find the right product for the customer and present the best possible deal before he leaves.

2. Then, he must develop and execute a follow-up plan designed to bring the opportunity back to close the sale, as well as to extend sales opportunities and build the relationship. Not only does this approach enable the salesperson to get the sale, but it also positions him to convert a customer to a client and to generate additional revenue and referral sales.

Creating Lasting Relationships

Of lost sales opportunities that leave a business without completing a transaction, 91% never receive a follow-up call or letter from the business, according to a J.D. Power study. That's nearly 100%, meaning salespeople are *almost perfect at not following up.* The biggest sales opportunity for every salesperson is picking up "lost" sales.

Smart sales teams view 100% of all opportunities that come to a business as buyers, even if they leave. Both the sales staff and store management must leverage established processes to develop follow-up plans for every opportunity based on their needs, wants, desires and other information gathered during their first visit. As new information becomes available that may help close a transaction, sales teams should contact the opportunities and bring them back to the store.

Automated systems give management the ability to check the status of every opportunity at any time. This ability ensures that "hot" opportunities won't turn cold. For example, it may be the store's policy that each salesperson sends an email and/or letter within 24-hours of the visit, the manager makes a follow-up call the next day, and the salesperson makes a confirmation call to set up a second visit within 48 hours. From the minute the opportunity leaves, the 72-hour clock begins to tick.

The Le Creuset cookware outlet store in the City of Industry, California, has this process mastered – unfortunately, it is not commonplace throughout the chain. Within 24 hours of a visit, each opportunity receives a thank you note, whether or not he has purchased. When items go on sale, the salespeople email or call their customers and clients, offer to set aside specific pieces and arrange a time to personally help them make final selections. When opportunities return they are greeted by name and won over as customers. Often recipes are shared that work well with previous or current purchases.

Once an opportunity is moved to a customer, the salesperson can develop a communication plan designed to build trust, convert him to a client and make incremental sales. Focusing on doing business and creating long-term clients can be a simple process if businesses and their sales teams adopt these basic practices:

1. Collect and record standardized, detailed data for every opportunity.

2. Present all the reasons why the opportunity should buy from the business.

3. Leverage technology to develop a follow-up action plan designed to bring the opportunity back and close the sale.

4. Focus on relationship building with existing customers with a goal of converting them to clients and generating additional revenue and referral sales.

5. Always leave the door open so that you can create a "be-back;" always give the customer a reason to return. Don't "slam" the door.

"Ninety percent of people say it should be easy to provide customer service, yet literally half the time they do not have a positive experience."

CHAPTER 6

MASTERING THE ART OF SELECTION: THE RED CARPET TREATMENT

Salespeople, who spend time learning about each individual customer's needs, wants, and desires, are helping customers make a selection that is exactly right for them. They involve the customer and work toward providing a quality selection, not toward closing a sale. With this approach, price – the primary roadblock to closing – becomes a distant consideration. These salespeople have transformed into Sales Selection Specialists who give *every* customer the "Red Carpet Treatment."

The Red Carpet Treatment, or treating the customer right, must always be the basis for the sales and service process. When sales and customer satisfaction go down, it is often because a business latched on to a new fad and forgot the business they were in, the business every company and organization must be in, the business of customer service.

Are your employees brimming with excitement and pride over the way they take care of your customers? When was the last time your customers were given the Red Carpet Treatment? Can't remember?

Ninety percent of people believe that it should be easy to provide customer service, yet literally half the time they do not have a positive experience, according to a survey by Creative Strategies and Connell Associates. The same study showed that 80% of people stopped doing business with a company because of bad service.

By going the extra mile, sales teams can create a positive buzz that keeps customers coming back. That extra effort is the best marketing any business or store could hope for and typically results in sales and referrals. By committing to extraordinary Red Carpet Treatment, sales managers can create a foundation for positive bottom line results and build loyal clientele.

Businesses and stores are often caught in a product trap; they're organized primarily around selling products rather than creating customers. Sales managers drive strategies and salespeople implement them. They talk about customer value instead of customized value. They fail to understand that there's a significant difference between the two: customer value is about delivering value to a general customer, but customized value is about selecting and delivering a solution for each client. That's the Red Carpet Treatment – individualized, exceptional service, every time.

Consumers tell us that they look for the "best price." Yet price alone does not sell a product; salespeople do. In APB's experience, we find that what consumers really want is to trust and have confidence in the salesperson and business or store where they shop. Building trust requires that salespeople take a genuine interest in their clientele.

Educating salespeople to help customers select an ideal product helps build that trust and confidence. It recognizes that the customer's perception must rank high in any successful and enduring sales approach. By taking a customer-centric approach, salespeople can spend as much time as possible learning about the customer's needs, wants and desires, and then discussing the product's features and benefits relative to those needs. This helps ensure that by the time price comes up, the customer is ready to buy.

Once your business commits to Red Carpet Treatment it can never stop. Let's look at Home Depot, for example. When the store first opened, it was structured specifically to offer the Red Carpet Treatment. Every employee made eye contact with each customer. When asked about a particular product, the salesperson would literally walk the customer to the aisle, point out the product, check to see if their needs were met, then quietly move on.

When the economy turned downward, Home Depot's attitude and product quality changed. Moving product quickly and managing expenses became more important than giving the Red Carpet Treatment. Employees' hours were slashed and benefits cut, causing a major shift in the attitude they adopted each day. This translated to their approach to customers until now it's difficult to find someone willing or knowledgeable enough to provide assistance. By focusing on product and bottom line, the company dishonored its brand and created an environment that became a self-fulfilling prophecy: the world is coming to an end and no one is buying.

In today's sales environment, the Red Carpet Treatment should be at the heart of every business strategy. Remember, the power in a sales relationship lies with the customer. Why wouldn't you want to treat them like royalty?

Sales managers committed to Red Carpet Treatment know that their service is only as good as their least engaged employee and that to give exceptional service requires a solid management structure and continuous education along with reward and motivation.

PART TWO:

BUILDING A SUCCESSFUL SALES ENVIRONMENT

"Accountability, consistency, communication and comprehension are essential ingredients to success in sales."

CHAPTER 7

THE CORNERSTONE OF SUCCESSFUL SELLING

A solid management structure is akin to the cornerstone of a strong building when it comes to developing successful sales teams and customer-centric environments. Without it, nothing else can be accomplished. Unless the cornerstone is supported by strong pillars – in this case Accountability, Consistency, Communication, and Comprehension – the entire structure is likely to collapse.

ACCOUNTABILITY

Typically, accountability strikes fear into the hearts of most people as it is most often used as a tool to track what is not being done! Yet, accountability works both ways and can give managers a clear view of their operations, and be used as a tool to measure and reward performance.

Everyone is accountable to someone in business, primarily to the person who pays the salary. In a sales organization, salespeople and managers are accountable to their customers and to the business that employs them. Sales managers must hold their salespeople accountable for customer interactions and their success in consistently executing the established process, in doing business the same way with each and every customer and client.

CONSISTENCY

Without consistency you have chaos. To eliminate the fear typically associated with accountability, sales managers must be absolutely consistent with every employee. First, there must be a consistent sales process in place to make sure that everyone is accountable for providing the Red Carpet Treatment:

1. Meet and greet the customer.

2. Ask the right questions.

3. Help the customer select the right product for their needs.

4. Collect specific information on every opportunity.

Every sales manager should hold every member of the sales team to the same standards consistently. Otherwise, measurements will result in a false perception of performance, and perception always becomes reality. Consistency means embracing one structure, one process and one means for holding everyone accountable every day with every person. Consistency, however, depends on clear communication and comprehension.

The Playing Field

Accountability

Consistency

Communication

Management Structure

Comprehension

COMMUNICATION

Communication about processes, expectations, and the day's game plan is an utter necessity for successful management. Successful communication is direct, clear, concise and easily understood. Once managers have a consistent plan, they should use sales meetings to communicate and set clear expectations. This can include specific tasks, but should focus on bringing consistency in how every salesperson follows the sales structure. When sales managers communicate clear, consistent performance metrics in advance to every employee, accountability becomes the expectation. It's important to note that sales meetings should be used only to educate, motivate, and inspire – in essence to create a positive environment for success. They should never be used to hold salespeople accountable, that should happen in a different time and place.

COMPREHENSION

The primary reason sales teams fear accountability is that they lack the understanding that equals comprehension of how to meet expectations or follow the game plan.

Individuals learn in three basic ways: hearing, seeing and experiencing. The best way for sales managers to ensure understanding is to explain an idea, model the behavior, and coach the salesperson as he works. Let's take prospecting as an example. A sales manager, who repeatedly tells his team to build the opportunity database by calling or pounding the pavement for new leads, most likely will not see positive results and will de-motivate his team when holding them accountable. The sales manager who makes the call while the salesperson observes or takes him to the local chamber mixer to network, then observes his salesperson's efforts and coaches for improvement, gives his people the skills needed to build their database and to succeed. It's like the adage: "Give a man a fish; you have fed him for today. Teach a man to fish; and you have taught him to prosper."

Successful sales managers embrace effective sales structures. They communicate and ensure comprehension of expectations by modeling, observing and coaching. They consistently apply processes and work with every salesperson in the same manner. They hold their teams accountable for the expectations that were communicated in a consistent manner. This sales structure is critical in any organization where the goal is to develop salespeople into true sales professionals.

"An accurate traffic count is required to effectively establish a performance baseline."

CHAPTER 8

MOTIVATING VS. DE-MOTIVATING

Despite their best efforts, many managers unknowingly de-motivate their teams. Looking solely at sales closed or meeting quotas as performance measures is one of the fastest ways do this. To drive positive attitudes and in turn drive business, changes need to start with management practices.

Let's begin with meetings. While most are intended to be motivational, they typically dwell on problems such as who forgot to restock or who left the keys out front or why numbers are down. Only at the end of the meeting is the team told to go out, have a great day and sell! Motivating or de-motivating? For most, they are completely de-motivating and contribute to negative attitudes. Instead, stores should hold motivational meetings.

First, set the tone of the meeting. Bring in bagels, cream cheese and coffee to help get the day started.

Second, set goals. Every manager should ask, "What will I teach my team in this meeting? How will I motivate them?" Review techniques and processes that help drive 100% results.

Third, cultivate a winning attitude. Talk about the positive aspects of the business or store and share stories about the difference that every salesperson can make in each customer's day simply by taking an interest and making each visit a pleasant experience.

One grocery store in Southern California, Gelsons, has mastered the art of motivating its teams, and it shows in the Red Carpet Treatment each customer receives. First they established a sales structure centered around customer service, which is clearly understood and consistently applied by every employee. Managers are visibly present modeling, observing and coaching. In addition, employees always present a positive attitude and are motivated to make certain that every customer's individual needs are taken care of.

At Gelsons, when customers asks where a product is located, the staff doesn't just tell them, they walk the customer to the exact location, ask what they are using it for, show the options for brands, sizes and flavors and then, once the client decides, they take it off the shelf and hand it to them. This store has made it clear that everyone is a salesperson from the cashier to the manager to the stock person. It's that level of effort that makes their clients willing to pay higher prices than those of the competition down the street.

Managers should recognize and reward this type of stellar performance by focusing on the team and giving everyone – not just "star performers" – a perk. In addition, rewards must be linked to the sales structure – the processes that must be consistently applied to deliver Red Carpet Treatment. Think about it, what does your organization do?

One frozen yogurt store in Atlanta, Yoforia, has a sales structure that emphasizes teamwork to ensure exceptional service. They reward their salespeople for extraordinary service, giving bonuses of up to $100.00 when they go out of their way to work closely with other employees to help their clients. This type of reward is available for every employee and helps set the positive tone that salespeople need to be successful and to work as a team.

—◆—

"When used effectively, motivation and incentives are powerful tools that can create positive attitudes, improve performance and add to the bottom line."

—◆—

Businesses of all types use sales contests to reward top performers, those who sell the most. Commissions are paid based on the number of units sold and any additional "incentive" is usually based on volume. Management perceives this as motivational while in reality, it is de-motivating for everyone except the top performers. To truly motivate and create a positive attitude throughout a sales team, contests and rewards must be based on the current performance level of every team member and recognize improved performance.

Before any contest or reward program can be used effectively, stores and businesses must have an accurate traffic count to establish a performance baseline.

Let's take two salespeople, as an example, Karen and Bill. In one week, Karen sold 20 televisions after talking to 150 opportunities and Bill sold eight televisions after working with 40 opportunities. Most would agree that Karen is the better salesperson because she sold more units. The reality is that Karen missed sales opportunities with 130 opportunities and achieved a closing rate of approximately 13% while Bill only missed opportunities with 32 opportunities and realized a 20% closing rate. Who did a better job?

Only when managers put units sold in the context of traffic count, can they accurately measure performance. Using these parameters, sales contests can be structured that reward an increase in performance – improving the close ratio. Not only does this reward the true performers, it motivates the entire team by creating a fair playing field. Do you know how much traffic –

how many opportunities – your business has every day? How many of those became customers or clients? How are you planning to close those that didn't?

When used effectively, motivation and incentives are powerful tools that can create positive attitudes, improve performance and add to the bottom line. They can be just as powerful in re-enforcing negative attitudes if improperly applied. To create the kind of positive attitude that encourages salespeople to see every opportunity that comes to a business or store as a potential customer or client, these tools must be applied consistently and fairly across the entire sales team.

"Customer service should become as routine as breathing, using a cell phone, or grabbing the first cup of coffee every morning."

CHAPTER 9

ARE YOU HANDLING CUSTOMERS OR MANAGING TRAUMAS?

Even with a solid sales structure in place, in the hustle and bustle of running a successful business, it's easy to get caught up in the mechanics of doing business and forget the reason for existing in the first place: customers and clients. When this happens, managers move into a reactive behavior and perform Customer Service Triage by racing from one trauma to another. Customer Service Triage is the process of sorting traumas into groups based on their likely benefit from immediate attention. It is exactly the opposite of where every manager wants to be.

By proactively performing regular Customer Service Check-ups, managers can ensure their customer handling processes are used consistently and properly, and that they are effective. In addition, these routine check-ups provide a unique means to check-in with customers and get first-hand feedback on how the business is really performing. After all, stores are in the business of helping people buy their products, not in the business of selling.

Minimally, Customer Service Check-ups should take place quarterly and cover every aspect of customer handling, from the moment an opportunity walks in, through the sales process to follow up. In essence, managers must ask, "Are we truly putting our greatest assets first?" These check-ups should be comprehensive, but not complex, and generally follow these six steps.

Step One: Are Customer Handling Processes And Excellence In Customer Service Part Of The Business Culture?

Every employee, starting with the highest level of management, must treat customer service as an integral part of his job. Customer service should become as routine as breathing, using a cell phone, or grabbing the first cup of coffee every morning. It doesn't have to be elaborate to make an impression, and often it's the small things that customers remember.

- A phone call returned on time

- A polite, sincere greeting and smile

- A card or email to mark a special occasion or a thank you note goes a long way

- A friendly greeting from every employee in every interaction

Every employee must go out of his way to make sure each customer feels welcome, on the phone, in person or online, even if the customer is working with someone else.

As part of the customer handling processes, be sure that standardized, detailed data is accurately collected and recorded for every customer. Schedule times/dates and the type of follow-up planned, using automated systems and verify that the processes are being followed.

"Minimally, Customer Service Check-ups should take place quarterly and cover every aspect of customer handling."

Step Two: Are We Responding Quickly And Personally To Every Customer?

Managers, sales teams and service personnel have the ability to respond quickly and personally to every customer.   Every employee should put themselves into his customers' shoes, imagine how he'd like to be treated, and then act accordingly. Are sales teams calling to check on his satisfaction with the business or to schedule a follow up appointment? Being proactive with customers is essential.

- Check established processes to be sure they are set up to capture every interaction so future inquiries can be responded to quickly and with accurate information.

- Disconnect the automatic response – every inquiry should be personalized and answered by an individual from the business, not by a machine.

- If you have no alternative, remember to KISS – Keep It Simple and Sincere. If your system directs callers to enter your extension then make sure your extension is everywhere – email signature, business cards, letterhead, etc.

- Test this system by sending an inquiry from a non-work email account or by calling from off-site.

Step Three: Do We Communicate Proactively With Our Customers?

Communication is essential to converting customers to clients and leveraging them as references. Keeping clients apprised of the status of their purchases – for example a product that has been ordered, or that is being repaired or upgraded – is critical. Client handling processes should clearly define steps to take if changes occur that potentially impact satisfaction.

- If a product or service is promised by a certain date and there are glitches, tell the client right away and tell him honestly what the status is.

- Automate systems to provide updates, news and other information.

- Be sure the current client data is on file and provides details that can be used to prospect based on family milestones where purchases may be considered such as a child's upcoming birthday or graduation.

Step Four: Are We Visibly And Continuously Appreciating Our Clients?

Client handling processes should show them that they are welcome and appreciated from the moment they are greeted through post-sales and service. Check to be sure that processes outline how to capture their data, identify their needs, and link them with an associate who can truly help them select and purchase the products or services they want. Do clients who come to the business feel welcome? While this seems obvious, many forget. As Voltaire said generations ago, "Common sense is not so common anymore."

- Provide simple amenities like coffee, water and a pleasant seating area.

- Keep a basket of toys handy for children who come along with their parents.

- Most important, thank them – for the visit, interest, time and sale. We can never thank clients enough for their business!

Step Five: Do We Ask Clients For Feedback And Act On It?

Check the processes that are designed to capture feedback from clients.

- Are you sending them postage-paid response cards or an email survey asking about their experience?

- How often is their input invited?

- What happens to the feedback that comes in?

- Are client appreciation functions like workshops and private showings scheduled?

- Is data from these events captured and used for additional feedback?

Do you accept the feedback without becoming defensive and use it to improve? Change the handling processes so they better meet the needs of all clients based on the direct feedback, and thank those who help you make a difference. After all, it's the clients' perception and perception *is* reality.

Step Six: Are We Continually Learning New Ways To Deliver Excellent Service?

Client service is every employee's responsibility. While managers can teach and demonstrate first-rate client service skills, excellence in service means understanding that everyone's primary responsibility is helping people select the right product, not simply selling. That's why it is essential to never stop learning.

Quarterly Customer Service Check-ups not only allow teams to evaluate their service and handling processes, but they enable teams to see if these processes are being used consistently. Armed with this data, teams can make intelligent decisions on how to improve the client experience instead of dealing with customer traumas.

"Everyone is in the customer service business."

CHAPTER 10

HAVE YOU LOOKED AT YOUR STORE THROUGH YOUR CUSTOMERS' EYES?

Think like your customer. Creating a "buyer-friendly" environment is one of the most important, ongoing programs a business can undertake to drive success and build clientele. Yet many of the initiatives designed to accomplish this become roadblocks that irritate, frustrate, and drive opportunities elsewhere. Take time to learn from first-hand experience by talking and *listening* to your customers.

The first step in creating a buyer-friendly business is to identify the roadblocks. Have you and your team shopped the store as if you were a potential buyer? If so, when was the last time? Observe the store's environment and interaction from this vantage point at least monthly. Call the business or store – what happens? Use the web site – is it buyer-friendly?

Some businesses hire "mystery shoppers" to report back to management after secretly shopping or discretely observing. There are two types of mystery shoppers. First, there are the "detectives" who are hired to spy on employees. Information from this source tells you little about how to improve processes and enhance the customer experience. Second, are the "observers," those who focus on finding out about the customer experience first-hand by "shopping" at a store or with a business. Their experiences provide invaluable insight into how every customer is treated and on which processes are effective.

Customers' perceptions are reality. By experiencing your business from the customers' vantage point, you will be equipped to refine processes and eliminate the roadblocks that discourage and frustrate customers and employees, and hinder your ability to convert customers to clients.

Equally important is listening to, observing and learning from the front-line salespeople and staff, those that talk to customers every day. Ask why they do things in a particular way and be open to learning from them. Most times, the adaptations they make to company processes result directly from their day-to-day customer interaction. More often than not, they enhance the customer experience.

Breaking Down Barriers

Working with businesses across the nation, I identified a number of barriers that are consistently cited by shoppers when asked what they find difficult about making a purchase. These include call screening, web site interaction and image.

Without exception, call screening, whether by an automated system or the receptionist, tops the list. When a shopper calls they often face an interrogation before being transferred, typically to an impersonal voicemail system. This is a true story I received by email from one of my readers:

> "I recently called a high line luxury business and asked for a salesperson. The receptionist asked me what product I was interested in. When I told her, she said that the person who handles that model was not in and offered to send me to voicemail, even though it was the last day of the month. I wondered if they were interested in selling or in finding ways not to sell."

We know who stopped this sale!

Worse yet is the situation where a buyer asks to speak to a manager, and rather than being transferred, is bombarded with questions or attempts at remedying the situation – which, at that point, is most likely unpleasant. This only causes more irritation and frustration and results in one of two scenarios: the buyer becomes a shopper or client of a competitor permanently, or the sales manager has to handle a Customer Trauma.

With an automated system the scene may play like this:

"Press one for sales, two for…"

"To check for store hours, press…"

Once transferred, the automation continues…"This is Pete, I can't take your call right now…"

For businesses and stores that rely on sales, and most do, **every** call is an **opportunity**. Any barrier, like call screening, should be eliminated. When a customer asks for a salesperson or s manager they should get one, immediately.

Not far behind call screening is complex web site interaction. Sales managers should navigate their site as if they were shoppers to determine how easy it is to use.

- Does every page display important information – especially the business or store phone number, street address and email – clearly and prominently? Why hide it?

- Are the pages uncluttered and well organized? If any page is too complex, viewers will abandon the site.

- Do the graphics reflect the brand image?

- Are tools that enable shoppers to conduct research, select and buy products or schedule service easily accessible?

- Is the email inquiry form straightforward or does it require a life history?

- Does an email generate an immediate, personal response from a salesperson the same day or the next morning if the inquiry comes in after business hours? Automated responses should be avoided at all costs.

- Do you offer a place where shoppers can interact and ask questions through email or live chat?

If these basics are not in place, your web site may be a barrier that prevents shoppers from visiting or purchasing.

While intangible, the image of the business, from the design and décor to the way employees dress, can be an asset or a barrier. A buyer is less apt to spend $40,000 on a luxury product with a salesperson dressed in a casual or overly worn outfit than with a salesperson that is professionally dressed. The same holds for a business with cluttered desks, dirty bathrooms or a chaotic environment versus a store that is pristine. Someone once said to me, "If the bathroom isn't clean, can you imagine what the kitchen looks like?" Consider this case in point.

The courthouse in Santa Monica, California, created a jury room designed to make a situation that most try to avoid, a pleasant and productive experience. The room has a private receptionist who is available to answer questions, provide recommendations for and directions to local restaurants and offer support to potential jurors. The area includes an outdoor balcony with several seating areas, a private "quiet room" for those wishing to nap, read, or work quietly, a television viewing room with options to accommodate several jurors, a kitchenette with microwave, sink, refrigerator and snack machines, computer and Wi-Fi access, and a main room where potential jurors can mingle and chat. Each area has plants and pleasant décor, and is kept neat and uncluttered.

This example underscores my previous statement that everyone is in the customer service business. The lesson for sales managers is to always dress your employees and your business for success.

Creating a customer-friendly environment is an ongoing process that should be measured and monitored monthly. It involves a commitment to continuous improvement and learning and to perpetual change. Unlike New Year's resolutions, habits are hard to break. Working with the end goal in mind, making it easy for customers to work with you, helps change habits and eliminate roadblocks. The devil is in the details.

"Consistent physical training and mental education will prepare individuals to size up the obstacle, understand how to approach it, and successfully overcome it."

CHAPTER 11

LESSONS FROM THE MUD RUN: WHAT IT TAKES TO WIN THE RACE

Every year thousands of individuals gather to compete in the "World Famous" Camp Pendleton Mud Run, a 10K run on the marine base that includes the kind of obstacles you'd encounter in basic training – a 30-foot mud pit, five-foot high walls, tires, river crossings, sand, tunnels and tough terrain. Repeatedly the top three teams are comprised of five high school boys. These teenage runners, who beat highly conditioned military competitors, don't simply show up and decide to run. They spend months preparing for the event, often running six days a week on routes that replicated the obstacles the course would hold. Through this, they learned a formula to help them face not only these obstacles, but also those they will face everyday throughout their lives.

What can we as sales professionals learn from this event and these teenagers? First, nothing stops an individual from reaching a goal except his own attitude and preparation. Second, the formula these teens learned embodies the four absolute necessities to achieving success:

1. Know the goal.
2. Know the obstacles.
3. Train, train, train = Educate.
4. Go back to basics.

Let's examine these individually as they apply to selling.

Know the goal. This is the ultimate first step. Without a clear understanding of the goal, it will never be achieved. In the teens' case the ultimate goal was to get through the obstacle course and come out healthy, unhurt and unscathed, and to win the race. For a business or store, the ultimate goal is to sell products or services and nurture clientele – people who will buy from you repeatedly and refer other opportunities. This goal, and others unique to each business and individual, must be clearly and consistently communicated to each salesperson.

Know the obstacles. In the Mud Run, the obstacles are similar, but can change year-to-year. This includes the physical obstacles on the course and the mental and physical obstacles unique to each athlete. The same is true in the selling. Obvious (physical) obstacles constantly change, but are similar and often cyclical. These can include technology advances, the fluctuating economy, a changing political environment, the housing crisis, changes in the weather and a host of other factors. Less apparent obstacles are unique to each salesperson. They range from attitude, prospecting skills, and using business procedures to the ability to help customers find the "perfect" product through closing the sale.

As managers, it's critical to understand both types of obstacles and their impact on each individual sales professional. Otherwise, this lack of understanding becomes an obstacle in itself, one that prevents the salespeople from addressing and overcoming all others. The challenge for sales managers is to identify the obstacles, and then consistently and repeatedly prepare their salespeople to overcome them before they greet the opportunity. The answer lies in the third lesson we can learn from the Mud Runners: training.

Train, train, train = Educate. Selling and running an obstacle course are very similar. Salespeople greet a customer; the runners go to the starting line. Salespeople introduce themselves, build a relationship and help the customer select a product; the runners take off and head for the finish line. Soon, both encounter the first obstacle. For the salesperson it may be, "I'm just looking;" for the runners, a five-foot wall. In each case, consistent physical training and mental education will prepare them to size up the obstacle, understand how to approach it, successfully overcome it, and proceed to the next part of the course (sale).

In the Mud Run, the teenagers prepared for a full year, for nearly 500 hours for this one event that lasted a mere 55 minutes. They knew the goal and the obstacles, trained and educated themselves consistently and repeatedly to meet them. Likewise, sales managers must constantly train and educate their salespeople to face the challenges presented by the prospective clients they face every day.

How long do you *really* train and educate your team before you let them work with customers in your business? Do you inspect their work every day to look for weakness and then provide continuous training and education for improvement? Training and education never stop as long as you're still in the race.

Training and education must be goal-based and must address obstacles faced both by teams and individuals. It should help salespeople learn to build clientele, individuals who rely on the business for an entire spectrum of products and services repeatedly and who refer friends, family and colleagues, not just sell one item. To do this, programs must teach salespeople to "sell" three things: themselves, the products and the business. I call this the three finger close. Without proper training and education, every salesperson risks turning opportunities into shoppers with every interaction.

Let's talk about basics. Everybody is always looking for the secret ingredient that magically turns opportunities to clients. Some are seduced by technology – Blackberries, Facebook or even Twitter. Others become seminar junkies looking for the latest get rich quick fad. These distractions only make salespeople forget the basics of selling. When that happens, sales suffer.

The basics of selling never change. They work day in and day out regardless of the economy or industry. Selling always hinges on helping the customer select the right product or service. Period. Converting customers to clients hinges on establishing a genuine relationship built on trust. Period. Remember, in sales, everything you do either adds to or detracts from your income.

Perhaps business and sales managers should look more closely at these teens. They chose not to simply play in the mud, but to set a goal, identify obstacles they would encounter, train, and educate, consistently and repeatedly to achieve their goal. The same is true for businesses that want to avoid playing in the muddy waters created by a whole range of obstacles. Their managers must clearly communicate the goal, help salespeople identify obstacles, and train and educate them to overcome all types of barriers to win the race.

One more lesson from these teens: Now that the race is won, what do you suppose they're doing? They are preparing for next year's race so they can get past new obstacles and continue to improve their performance, and win. Are you ready to win?

"Having a career path is part of the route to longevity and retention."

CHAPTER 12

IS YOUR BUSINESS "PEOPLE BROKE?"

Many businesses are not *money broke* today, they are *"people broke."*

Businesses spend hundreds of thousands of dollars yearly in advertising and promotions to drive opportunities into their stores only to realize – too late – that they don't have the team in place to serve these potential customers as they arrive. Many businesses have the money and resources, but don't make the commitment to continually educate their teams. They fail to realize that you can have the best product or service, the best brand, or even a solid structure, but that without well-educated people they may as well be broke.

Being "people broke" is a critical limiting factor for growth as businesses look to expand and acquire additional stores. This applies not only to salespeople, but also to every employee – managers, buyers, greeters, cashiers, assistants – everyone.

So, how can you overcome being "people broke" and focus on growth and expansion? The solution can be broken down into three areas:

1. Develop people from within.

2. Offer a career opportunity for every employee.

3. Equip employees with the tools they need to succeed.

Develop People From Within

When businesses look externally to fill sales or management positions, they typically recruit from a pool of professionals employed at other like businesses in the general vicinity. When this happens, the new recruits bring the methods and habits of their former employer to their new position whether or not these methods and habits match the established processes and culture of their new employer.

In essence, it's a double-edged sword. The new manager is hired to run the organization based on their past successes, yet he is expected to do so within the parameters of an established structure, which he doesn't understand. As a result, the new manager changes the structure. This may result in a temporary increase in performance and business; however, since the rest of the team is not trained and has not bought-in to the new structure, the long-term impact is a performance drop and an increase in turn-over. I call this the "Flash In The Pan" – the new managers come in throw some fuel on the fire resulting in a big flash, which then burns out quickly.

Conversely, when businesses hire – or promote – someone from within, the process becomes much simpler with better results. For example, when someone is promoted from a sales position into a sales manager position, the individual already knows the structure; the way the business operates and the processes used; the values of the organization, what the business stands for and everything else about the way it does business. When promoted from within, the new manager is not intent on changing things. He is ready to take the next step in the established structure, using processes that are familiar to the entire team, to continue to drive growth and performance.

"Building longevity – not simply retaining employees – requires a different mindset beginning at the highest level."

Where Is My Opportunity?

Within an established structure with clearly defined processes, it is essential to provide teams with a clear career path. Structure develops people, yourself and everyone around you. Nothing is stronger than having a structure in place. Having a career path not only clearly demonstrates the opportunities they have with the business, but also creates a team environment where everyone shares a common culture and goals. To complement a career path, businesses must offer an attractive employment package – a longevity plan that serves as an incentive for employees to stay. This can include health insurance, life insurance, spousal benefits and the possibility for substantial financial gain regardless of the position an employee holds.

Equip Employees With The Tools To Succeed

Having a career path is only part of the route to longevity and retention. It is essential that businesses help their people develop. To do so, businesses must provide mandatory education in the skills needed for every job function for every employee. Educational programs cannot be offered selectively for several reasons:

1. Education builds an understanding that part of each person's job is to nurture and develop people below them – and education gives them the skills to do so.

2. Education gives every employee the same ability to embrace new skills and apply them in new ways on an even playing field.

3. A star performer may emerge only after he receives the education and tools needed for success.

4. Conversely, a "superstar" in his current role may not have the mindset or ability to embrace the skills needed to advance, a fact that will become clear as education is provided.

Educational programs don't have to be complex, but must be comprehensive and ongoing. They must include motivational, organizational, managerial, sales, service and leadership skills.

Building longevity – not simply retaining employees – requires a different mindset beginning at the highest level. In this model, employees are viewed as an asset, not an expense. Education, career paths and longevity programs are seen as investments with the potential for high returns – profits and growth. Using this model, businesses can create an environment that makes them "people rich" and that leads to high financial returns.

"Education not only makes it clear that part of each team member's job is to help his teammates, it teaches him how."

GET IN SHAPE
FOR THE BIG GAME

Everyone loves football season, especially in New England where I live – and why not? Football has entertained us, given us terrific memories, brought forth role models, and shown us the meaning of practice, commitment and team work. So, with a little help from Vince Lombardi's wisdom and Bill Belichick's insight, let's examine what football can teach us about the retail business.

> *"Practice does not make perfect.*
> *Only perfect practice makes perfect."*
>
> *Vince Lombardi, Coach, Green Bay Packers*

Just ask the New England Patriots, winners of three of the seven Super Bowls they've played. This team, like all others, spends days analyzing their opponents, looking at game films, and preparing to play. They practice and study six days a week, eight hours a day or more to execute a game plan or play four times each month in a 60 minute game. Even players who have held the same position for 15 years strive to get stronger and smarter so they can help the team win. These players know that it's not always the team with the biggest and fastest players that win. The winning team is the one that is best prepared and best executes its game plan. As a team they've developed a mindset that can overcome physical obstacles, help maintain focus, and ensure the plan is executed flawlessly.

How does this compare with an average store? In the retail automotive business, for example, salespeople are expected to work 40, maybe 50 hours a week, and to interact with 50 to 60 customers per month. But, when it comes to practices, most stores are far from perfect. The time to practice is not when the customer arrives. Stores should practice – delivering education, developing skills and honing talent – a minimum of 30 minutes a day, Monday through Friday, with their teams.

> *"Confidence is contagious and so is lack of confidence, and a customer will recognize both."*
> *Vince Lombardi, Coach, Green Bay Packers*

Like football teams, store teams must clearly understand the game plan including processes, techniques and goals, and have confidence in their ability to execute it as a team. Stores are obliged to provide education in the skills needed for every job function for every employee. Education not only makes it clear that part of each team member's job is to help his teammates, but also teaches him how.

Similarly, delineating the store's vision, processes, and procedures gives every employee the same chance to embrace new skills and apply them in new ways as a team. Often, education uncovers star performers who emerge only after they receive the tools and information they need to succeed. Educational programs don't have to be complex, but must be comprehensive and include motivational, organizational, managerial, sales, service and leadership skills.

> *"Life's battles don't always go to the stronger or faster man. But sooner or later the man who wins, is the man who thinks he can."*
>
> *Vince Lombardi, Coach, Green Bay Packers*

On Saturday, "game day" in the business world, and typically the busiest day of the week, the 30 minutes should be inspirational, devoted to motivating the team to succeed. Focus on the positive aspects of the store and the team's accomplishments. Surprise everyone – not just the "stars" – with a gift certificate to the movies or a coffee store. Motivational meetings set the stage for nurturing an upbeat attitude and help salespeople execute on the game plan they've practiced all week.

> *"On a football team, it's not the strength of the individual players, but it is the strength of the unit and how they all function together."*
>
> *Bill Belichick, Coach, New England Patriots*

So, practice, educate, motivate, execute, encourage teamwork, and inspire to win! It's not just a game, it's a learning experience.

"Ongoing education represents an opportunity to grow people, profit, and performance."

CHAPTER 14

EDUCATING PROFESSIONALS FOR SUCCESS: A LIFELONG PROCESS

What is the difference between education and training?

Education develops the faculties and powers of (a person) by teaching, instruction, or schooling; to qualify by instruction or training for a particular calling, practice, etc. It focuses on the individual and his ability to make a contribution.*

Training gives the discipline and instruction, drill, practice, etc., designed to impart proficiency or efficiency. It focuses on a specific, finite task.*

Let's take a closer look at how education builds from one level to the next:

- Pre-school – provides a good foundation in personal, social and emotional development, knowledge, and creativity that enables individuals to become more confident and able and ready to learn much more as the years go by.

- Elementary School – achieves the best possible intellectual, moral, social, and physical development of the individual while developing the potential of each person and preparing him for the responsibilities and fulfillment of adulthood.

- Middle School – introduces a broader range of exploratory courses and activities in order to assist young adolescents to discover and develop their interests and abilities through teacher-advisor programs, extracurricular activities, and core curriculum.

- High School – prepares students for a meaningful life; to be a good citizen, economically self-sufficient, and respectful of themselves and others; to ensure that all students leave ready for college, jobs and/or civic involvement.

- College/University – takes middle school and high school imparted knowledge to the next level, prepares individuals to specialize in a particular field and empowers the student with life skills that enable him to contribute positively to society.

- Post-graduate Study – provides advanced learning in specialized disciplines, an in-depth understanding such that the student becomes something of an expert in the topic of study; prepares students for today's diverse careers in the public and private sector, or for continued study.

Education should never stop, yet, in the sales profession, the focus has shifted to training, and minimal training at best. New hires are typically given collateral, a video, an office tour, and introductions, shown their desk, phone, and order pad, and expected to jump in.

To augment this, sales trainers are continually advocating new techniques, workshops, and seminars, all designed to provide quick fixes that will jump start sales. I call that "flash in the pan" training. These fixes simply offer a brief burst in sales that dies out just as fast. In fact, when analyzed over a two month period, these bursts only move business from one month to another. The two-month average stays the same. It seems like everyone is always looking for something new without having mastered the basics. Until 100% of the customers coming in get the Red Carpet Treatment, no one will have earned the right to "try something new."

The bottom line is that retail teams don't need training to succeed. They need education, an ongoing process of growth that builds on previous lessons and provides structure, but that never ends.

Professional education is a lifelong process that should be facilitated by every business and embraced by every employee, from manager to receptionist. Every day something new emerges that requires learning and has applications for business. Today it's YouTube, Twitter, Facebook, Instagram, an "app for that" and on and on. People can get virtually anything, anytime, anywhere. When individuals stop learning they stop growing. In sales, those who stop growing are quickly left behind.

Ongoing education is an investment not an expense. No longer can a business capture a good share of the market simply by having a quality product. Businesses need to find ways to separate their operations from their competition. Good service and properly trained people certainly are the top ways to get that done.

At the "pre-school" level, professionals are generally new to the industry and require training in the basics including:

- Introduction – hours of operation, technology and tools available, iPads, CRM, etc.

- Sales orientation (product/service training)

- Sales administration – resources at your disposal

- Business culture and guiding principles

- Job description – not selling, but helping customers select the exact product or service that fits their needs

- The processes unique to the business including the methods used to greet and capture important data from every customer

As employees advance, their progress should be monitored against clearly established and communicated goals. If challenges arise, they should be viewed as indications of the need for additional education in a particular area that can complement ongoing education. More advanced programs allow individuals to hone their skills or concentrate on specific areas. These may include education in:

- Key account management
- Customer service excellence
- Sales
- Telephone skills
- Telephone sales
- Sales management
- Prospecting

- Customer relationship management
- Negotiation skills

As managers, it's important to quickly gain an understanding of what level each employee is at, from "elementary to post-graduate." With this understanding, managers can provide educational opportunities that build on each employee's existing knowledge.

The Red Carpet Treatment must always be the basis for the sales and service process. When sales and customer satisfaction go down, it is often because the business tried something new and forgot the basics. A consistent process helps companies keep to the fundamentals and establishes measurements to identify ways to improve.

Education is also essential for the leaders who have learned the importance of providing the resources needed to get the job done and who concentrate on becoming their best – not on trying to beat their competition. These leaders must become personally involved and demonstrate the value of education in ways that their people can understand. Managers must demonstrate by example the lessons taught to every employee and set the tone that everyone can follow. When they do, they will be supported by an army of well-educated staff that executes on the lessons they've learned.

Ongoing education represents an opportunity to grow people, profit and performance. Companies should prioritize investment – people first, then capital improvements. Buildings don't sell products or services, people do. Until business leaders embrace that philosophy, they will always be a step behind. Businesses today aren't "money broke," they are "people broke."

*Source: Dictionary.com

---

*"Learning not to
stop the sale is a process."*

CHAPTER 15

ARE YOU
STOPPING THE SALE?

If you answered no to this question then you might consider reading this book again. Everyone at some time stops the sale; they just don't realize they are doing it.

Learning *not* to stop the sale is a process, and like preparing for a football game or mud run, it takes practice. It starts every day when you choose what attitude you will bring to every situation you encounter throughout the day. If you give 100% Attitude, 100% Effort and 100% Performance, you will get 100% Results.

Listen to your customers, intently and genuinely. Help them find the right solution, whether they purchase today or in several weeks. Treat each opportunity like royalty, like you'd want to be treated, and give them a positive experience they'll never forget. Take every chance you can to build trust and cultivate clients for life. Nurture and inspire those around you because your success is intimately intertwined with the success of your coll

The information in this book is proven to work, but only when embraced with an open mind and the understanding that success in sales is a process nurtured by continuous learning and improvement. The *Who Stopped the Sale?* Toolbox that follows includes some quick tips and tools to help you monitor your progress and succeed on your journey.

The first step is being willing to admit that you, too, stop sales. Step two? Recognize that ultimately, your job is not to sell customers something; your job is to help them buy.

WHO STOPPED THE SALE?

TOOLBOX

DO	DON'T
Decide to bring a positive attitude daily	Whine
Set specific goals and be accountable	Come in without a plan or you will be planning to fail!
Eliminate "no, don't, won't, can't" from your vocabulary	Give customers reasons not to buy
Ask questions	Ask questions unless you know the answer
Listen for needs, wants, desires	Sell what's on hand
Help customers buy	Sell
Give everyone the Red Carpet Treatment	Judge people by their looks or questions
Give the customer a reason to buy from you and your business	Focus on selling *NOW*
Focus on relationships	Take people for granted
Convert the customer to a client	Drop the relationship after the sale closes
Prospect to find the next opportunity	Rely solely on advertising
Continually educate yourself	Assume you know it all
Turn buyers into shoppers	Focus on selling *NOW*

Self-assessment

Be honest, how would you rate yourself on the following statements – rarely, sometimes or usually?

1. I come to work with a positive attitude every day.

2. I view every person that walks into my business or calls as an opportunity.

3. I actively listen to learn what each client is looking for.

4. I anticipate questions.

5. I make relevant suggestions.

6. I help customers select the right solution or product.

7. I make every client feel like a VIP by giving them the Red Carpet Treatment.

8. I set measureable goals and hold myself accountable for achieving them.

9. I am knowledgeable about my products or services.

10. I focus on continuous education for improvement.

11. I work as part of a team.

12. I inspire others to excel.

13. I convert every opportunity into loyal clients.

If you answered sometimes or rarely to any statement, there is room for improvement. Set goals, seek out new information and practice every day. In a few weeks repeat this assessment. Remember, learning not to stop the sale is an ongoing process.

KEYS TO SUCCESS

S	**Single-mindedness**	The salesperson's job is to help find the right product and the right price for each individual customer. By keeping this in mind, setting, and monitoring goals and objectives as part of a daily routine, he can develop a single-mindedness that brings focus and ultimately success.
U	**Understanding**	Having a deep understanding of the job and the product or service is often taken for granted. Salespeople must include time in their daily plans to follow consumer buying trends and news that can impact their clientele. They must learn about what drives sales, why individuals purchase, and the challenges and concerns that create obstacles to closing deals.
C	**Continuous Learning**	In the sales business, there is no "status quo." Education must be a constant goal. Successful salespeople seek opportunities to learn from each encounter every day with customers, friends, family, and colleagues. They study market trends, competitive offerings, and new products and services and equip themselves with the knowledge needed to become valued resources to their clients.
C	**Curiosity**	Curiosity and enthusiasm spark interest. With technical advancements, constantly changing products, services, and practices, it is easy to be overwhelmed. An active curiosity helps salespeople keep up with these developments. In addition, curiosity is a useful tool when it comes to asking clients the right questions. An enthusiastic, curious salesperson can easily learn about a client's needs, wants, and desires, all critical information required to help spark excitement and find customers' the right product or service.
E	**Empathy**	Empathy is the ability to understand the customers' problems from their point of view. Salespeople must take the time to identify with each customer's concerns in a genuine manner and walk in their shoes, if they want to meet or exceed expectations, and ultimately succeed themselves.
S	**State-of-Mind**	A positive state-of-mind or attitude is critical, regardless of the individuals, circumstances, or tenor of the day. A positive attitude keeps salespeople focused on their clientele, and can turn a potentially negative customer or situation into a positive outcome and even a sale.
S	**Structure**	Structure helps every member of a team ensure not only their own success, but also the success of a business or store. If team members rely on established processes that help them to develop plans, work in tandem with their teammates, and support each other's efforts, then success is surely the only possible result.

Notes

Questions or comments?
Contact me at rlibin@apb.cc

NOTES

_____

_____

_____

_____

_____

_____

_____

_____

_____

_____

Questions or comments?
Contact me at rlibin@apb.cc

NOTES

_____

_____

_____

_____

_____

_____

_____

_____

_____

_____

_____

Questions or comments?
Contact me at rlibin@apb.cc

ABOUT THE AUTHOR

Richard F. Libin, president of Automotive Profit Builders, Inc. (APB), is focused on ensuring that the management and staff of its clients keep pace with today's sophisticated and more demanding consumers, while excelling in customer satisfaction. Through more than 30 years of experience, Mr. Libin has come to believe that education must be a long-term investment not an expense; that no longer can a business capture a good share of the market simply by having a quality product. His leadership in adapting new technologies for improved sales and service performance has helped thousands of businesses differentiate their operations from their competition, maximize profits, and develop their people.

Mr. Libin is a sought-after author who writes regular articles for industry trade media and professional association publications. He is a frequent speaker at industry conventions and association meetings, and conducts a regular schedule of classes through APB Sales University.